THE 12 DAYS OF CHRISTMAS
AN ILLUSTRATED CAROL

Taama Marti Forasiepi

THANKS

This book was developed over a 2 year period. It started as a series of panels I intended to use as Christmas cards. But as time passed my friends and family encouraged me to also make it a book. Each panel came to life over coffee, vacations, traveling, and in my studio. One very special panel (two turtle doves) was finished while waiting in the lobby for the birth of my business partner's first child.

I wish to thank all who listened, reviewed and encouraged me. I'd like to offer a very special thanks to my husband of 30 years, John, who supports me in all of my endeavors. Thanks to my business partner, David Brehm, and his wonderful wife, Stephanie, for your encouragement and support. And finally, a thanks rings out to my focus group, Charles Harris, and Millard Almon, for their unwavering support and helpful reviews.

Artwork copyright © 2015 Taama Marti Forasiepi
All rights reserved.

Published by Sans Soucie Studio, Dallas, Texas.

ISBN: 978-0-692-59323-3

Edited and illustrated by Taama Marti Forasiepi

No part of this publication may be reproduced, stored in a retrieval system, or transmitted in any form or by any means, electronic, mechanical, photocopying, recording, scanning, or otherwise, except with the written permission of the Publisher.

Printed in the United States of America.

PREFACE

Some say that the Christmas carol, "The 12 Days of Christmas", was used during an era in history when Catholics were forbidden to practice openly and it may have served as a secret way to teach children about the Catechism. Others refer to the song as merely a childhood memory development tool. The song becomes progressively more difficult as one advances through the lyrics, remembering what has been and what is to come.

Whatever the historical use may have been, "The 12 Days of Christmas" has remained one of my favorite holiday carols. However, it is one of the most misunderstood carols of the season. The confusion is because the "12 days" does not refer to the days before Christmas, but instead to the "12 days" after Christmas. The song culminates on January 5th, the day before the Epiphany.

A Partridge sitting quietly in a pear tree starts the tune. Each scene grows in the number of animals set comfortably in a serene setting. The number eight becomes a transition from animals to people; from nature to civilization. The song carries us from rural living to intricate social endeavors. The dancing ladies and leaping lords allow us to frolic in the celebration of music. We are serenaded by the pipers and the song culminates with the triumphant drummers.

*On the first day of Christmas
my true love gave to me:*
A partridge in a pear tree.

*On the second day of Christmas
my true love gave to me:*
Two turtle doves
and a partridge in a pear tree.

*On the third day of Christmas
my true love gave to me:*
Three french hens,
*two turtle doves,
and a partridge in a pear tree.*

*On the fourth day of Christmas
my true love gave to me:*
Four calling birds,
*three french hens,
two turtle doves,
and a partridge in a pear tree.*

*On the fifth day of Christmas
my true love gave to me:*
Five golden rings,
*four calling birds,
three french hens,
two turtle doves,
and a partridge in a pear tree.*

*On the sixth day of Christmas
my true love gave to me:*
Six geese a laying,
*five golden rings,
four calling birds,
three french hens,
two turtle doves,
and a partridge in a pear tree.*

*On the seventh day of Christmas
my true love gave to me:*
Seven swans a swimming,
*six geese a laying,
five golden rings,
four calling birds,
three french hens,
two turtle doves,
and a partridge in a pear tree.*

*On the eighth day of Christmas
my true love gave to me:*
Eight maids a milking,
*seven swans a swimming,
six geese a laying,
five golden rings,
four calling birds,
three french hens,
two turtle doves,
and a partridge in a pear tree.*

*On the ninth day of Christmas
my true love gave to me:*
Nine ladies dancing,
*eight maids a milking,
seven swans a swimming,
six geese a laying,
five golden rings,
four calling birds,
three french hens,
two turtle doves,
and a partridge in a pear tree.*

*On the tenth day of Christmas
my true love gave to me:*
Ten lords a leaping,
*nine ladies dancing,
eight maids a milking,
seven swans a swimming,
six geese a laying,
five golden rings,
four calling birds,
three french hens,
two turtle doves,
and a partridge in a pear tree.*

*On the eleventh day of Christmas
my true love gave to me:*
Eleven pipers piping,
*ten lords a leaping,
nine ladies dancing,
eight maids a milking,
seven swans a swimming,
six geese a laying,
five golden rings,
four calling birds,
three french hens,
two turtle doves,
and a partridge in a pear tree.*

*On the twelfth day of Christmas
my true love gave to me:*
Twelve drummers drumming,
*eleven pipers piping,
ten lords a leaping,
nine ladies dancing,
eight maids a milking,
seven swans a swimming,
six geese a laying,
five golden rings,
four calling birds,
three french hens,
two turtle doves,
and a partridge in a pear tree.*

www.ingramcontent.com/pod-product-compliance
Lightning Source LLC
Chambersburg PA
CBHW061818290426
44110CB00026B/2908